The Wonderful Autistic Brain:

How To Connect and Empower Neurodiverse People

"Autism is a way of being, not something to be fixed." -

Gretchen Branson (advocate for autism acceptance)

Introduction

- Hey there! Have you ever wondered what it's like to live with autism? This book isn't just about explaining it, it's about celebrating the amazing strengths of autistic people.

- We'll talk about how their brains work differently, which can lead to incredible focus, a hawk-eye for detail, and super creative problem-solving skills. Plus, we'll explore some tips for communication and creating supportive environments so everyone can thrive.

- Think of it as a guide to understanding and appreciating the unique talents autistic people bring to the world. It's gonna be eye-opening!

Contents

Part 1: Understanding and Celebrating the Wonderful Autistic Brain

- Chapter 1: What is Autism Spectrum Disorder?

- Chapter 2: The Wonderful Autistic Brain: Strengths and Unique Perspectives

  1. Autistic Strengths
  2. Unique perspectives: Passion and Focus, Honesty and Integrity, Attention to Detail, Strong Memories

- Chapter 3: Autism Facts and Anatomy (Optional): You can combine these chapters if the anatomy section is brief.

  1. Interesting Facts about Autism
  2. (Optional) The Neurological Basis of Autism (Brief overview)

- Chapter 4: Wonderful Things About Autism: Reframe challenges as strengths.

Part 2: Communication and Connection for Neurodiverse People

- Chapter 5: Signs and Symptoms of Autism Spectrum Disorder (ASD)

Contents

- **Chapter 6: The Diagnostic Process for ASD: Early Intervention and Getting Help**

- **Chapter 7: Understanding Nonverbal Communication for the Autistic Brain**

Part 3: Empowering Neurodiverse People: Social Skills, Emotional Management, and Self-Care

- **Chapter 8: The Importance of Social Skills and How They Develop**

- **Chapter 9: Strategies for Developing Social Skills in Autistic People**

1. How the Autistic Brain Understands Social Cues (tailored to this audience)

- **Chapter 10: Managing Feelings in the Autistic Brain: Emotional Regulation Strategies**

- **Chapter 11: Physical Self-Care for Autistic People**

1. Movement and Sensory Regulation
2. Stimulating the Vagus Nerve for Calming and Focus

Contents

- **Chapter 12: Healthy Nutrition for Autistic People**

  1. Creating a Balanced Diet
  2. Essential Vitamins and Minerals
  3. The Importance of Omega-3s, Magnesium, and Vitamin B6
  4. Dietary Sources of Protein, Fiber, and Calcium

Part 4: Expanding Language Skills in the Autistic Brain

- **Chapter 13: Strategies to Enhance Language Skills**

- **Chapter 14: Understanding Language Processing in the Autistic Brain:**

  1. Discuss potential challenges with language processing, such as auditory processing difficulties or literal interpretations.
  2. Explain different learning styles that may be present in autistic individuals.

Contents

- **Chapter 15: Building a Strong Foundation for Language Development:**

1. Focus on early intervention strategies for children with ASD.
2. Discuss the importance of receptive language skills and how to develop them.
3. Cover foundational skills like building vocabulary, using simple sentence structures, and improving communication clarity.

- **Chapter 16: Developing Conversational Skills:**

1. Break down the components of successful conversation for the autistic brain.
2. Offer strategies for initiating and maintaining conversations, including turn-taking and active listening skills.
3. Discuss techniques for understanding nonverbal cues and using them appropriately in conversation.

Conclusion

Part 1: Understanding and Celebrating the Wonderful Autistic Brain

Chapter 1: What is Autism Spectrum Disorder?

Part 1: Understanding and Celebrating the Wonderful Autistic Brain
Chapter 1: What is Autism Spectrum Disorder?

Autism Spectrum Disorder (ASD) is a complex developmental disorder that affects how a person perceives and interacts with the world around them. It's characterized by a combination of challenges in three main areas:

- **Social communication and interaction:** People with ASD may have difficulty understanding nonverbal cues like facial expressions and body language. They may also find it hard to take turns in conversation, understand jokes or sarcasm, or make friends.

- **Restricted interests and repetitive behaviors:** People with ASD may have intense interests in specific topics and engage in repetitive behaviors, such as lining things up, hand flapping, or following strict routines.

- **Sensory processing:** Some people with ASD may experience sensory overload, where sights, sounds, smells, or touches feel overwhelming. Others may under-respond to sensory stimuli.

It's important to remember that autism is a spectrum disorder, so the way it manifests can vary greatly from person to person. Some people with ASD may be very high-functioning and able to live independently, while others may need more support.

Part 1: Understanding and Celebrating the Wonderful Autistic Brain
Chapter 1: What is Autism Spectrum Disorder?

Here are some additional points to consider:

- Symptoms typically appear by age 2 or 3.
- There is no cure for autism, but there are treatments that can help people with ASD manage their symptoms and live fulfilling lives.
- Early intervention is crucial for maximizing a person's potential.

Part 1: Understanding and Celebrating the Wonderful Autistic Brain
Chapter 2: The Wonderful Autistic Brain: Strengths and Unique Perspectives
2.1- Autistic Strengths

Autistic people possess a range of strengths that can be truly remarkable. Here are some of the most common ones:

- **Attention to Detail:** They often have a keen eye for detail and can excel at tasks requiring precision and focus. This can be a huge asset in fields like science, engineering, art, and music.

- **Strong Memories:** Many autistic individuals have exceptional memories, allowing them to retain vast amounts of information on topics of interest. This can be a superpower for trivia buffs, data analysts, and anyone needing to remember complex details.

- **Logical Thinking:** Autistic brains often excel at logical reasoning and problem-solving. They can approach challenges systematically and identify creative solutions. This strength shines in mathematics, computer programming, and any field requiring analytical thinking.

- **Passion and Focus:** When autistic people find a topic they're passionate about, they can devote intense focus and energy to learning everything they can about it. This deep focus can lead to expertise and innovation in various fields.

Part 1: Understanding and Celebrating the Wonderful Autistic Brain
Chapter 2: The Wonderful Autistic Brain: Strengths and Unique Perspectives
2.1- Autistic Strengths

- **Honesty and Integrity:** Many autistic individuals value truthfulness and fairness. They may be less likely to engage in social deception and can be highly reliable. This is a valuable asset in building trust and strong relationships.

- **Unique Perspectives:** Their way of perceiving the world can be different, leading to unique insights and creative approaches. This can be a game-changer in art, design, and any field that benefits from unconventional thinking.

- **Visual Thinking:** Many autistic people think visually and excel at processing information presented visually. This can be a strength in graphic design, architecture, and fields that rely heavily on visual representation.

- **Rule-Following:** People with autism often thrive on routine and predictability. Their adherence to rules can make them dependable and meticulous, which is valuable in many professions.

It's important to remember that these strengths will vary from person to person. Some individuals may possess several of these strengths, while others may have more prominent ones unique to them. The key is to identify and nurture these strengths to help autistic people reach their full potential.

Part 1: Understanding and Celebrating the Wonderful Autistic Brain
Chapter 2: The Wonderful Autistic Brain: Strengths and Unique Perspectives

2.2- Unique perspectives: Passion and Focus, Honesty and Integrity, Attention to Detail, Strong Memories

These are all fantastic strengths that contribute to the "Unique perspectives" found in many autistic individuals. Here's a breakdown of how each one can lead to a unique way of seeing and interacting with the world:

Passion and Focus:

- **Deep Dives:** Autistic people's intense focus allows them to delve deeply into specific subjects, often uncovering hidden connections or details others might miss. This can lead to groundbreaking discoveries and innovative solutions.

- **Unconventional Approaches:** Unbound by traditional methods, their passion can fuel them to explore problems from entirely different angles, leading to unexpected breakthroughs.

Honesty and Integrity:

- **Unfiltered Observations:** Their direct communication style can provide a refreshingly honest perspective, free from social biases or sugarcoating. This can be invaluable in situations requiring objective evaluation.

- **Focus on Fairness:** Their strong sense of justice can lead them to question the status quo and advocate for fair treatment, fostering a more inclusive and equitable environment.

Part 1: Understanding and Celebrating the Wonderful Autistic Brain
Chapter 2: The Wonderful Autistic Brain: Strengths and Unique Perspectives

2.2- Unique perspectives: Passion and Focus, Honesty and Integrity, Attention to Detail, Strong Memories

Attention to Detail:

- **"Big Picture" Through Details:** Their ability to notice intricate details allows them to see the bigger picture from a unique vantage point. They can identify subtle patterns or inconsistencies that others might overlook.

- **Enhanced Sensory Perception:** For some autistic individuals, heightened sensitivity to sights, sounds, or textures can lead to a richer and more nuanced understanding of their surroundings.

Strong Memories:

- **Vivid Recall:** Their exceptional memories can provide them with a vast repository of information and experiences, allowing them to draw connections across seemingly disparate concepts.

- **Preserving History and Tradition:** Their ability to retain details can be crucial for preserving historical information, cultural traditions, or endangered languages.

These strengths, combined with other autistic traits, create a unique lens through which autistic people experience the world. They can be powerful tools for innovation, problem-solving, and fostering a more diverse and understanding society.

Part 1: Understanding and Celebrating the Wonderful Autistic Brain
Chapter 3: Autism Facts and Anatomy :
3.1- Interesting Facts about Autism

Here are some interesting facts about Autism Spectrum Disorder (ASD) that you might not know:

- **Early Signs:** The first signs of autism can appear in children as early as 12 months old. However, a diagnosis is typically not confirmed until age 2 or 3.

- **The Gender Gap**: Boys are diagnosed with ASD about 4 times more often than girls. However, some experts believe this gap may be due to under-diagnosis in females who may mask symptoms better.

- **The Savant Skill:** While not everyone with autism has them, some autistic people possess extraordinary talents or skills in specific areas, known as savant skills. These can include exceptional memory, advanced musical ability, or profound artistic talent.

- **More Than Meets the Eye:** People with autism may experience the world differently due to sensory processing differences. They might find certain sounds overwhelming or textures unpleasant, while others might crave deep pressure or enjoy repetitive visual stimuli.

Part 1: Understanding and Celebrating the Wonderful Autistic Brain
Chapter 3: Autism Facts and Anatomy:
3.1- Interesting Facts about Autism

The Language Link: Not everyone with autism has difficulty speaking. In fact, some autistic people develop advanced vocabularies in their areas of interest. However, challenges with social communication are a hallmark feature of ASD and can affect how they use language in social contexts.

Autistic and Artistic: Many people with autism excel in artistic fields like music, art, and literature. Their unique perspectives and detail-oriented nature can lead to the creation of profoundly moving and innovative works.

The Global Community: Autism affects people of all races, ethnicities, and socioeconomic backgrounds. It's estimated to occur in roughly 1 in 44 children in the United States.

The Tech Connection: There appears to be a link between autism and certain technical skills. People with autism may be drawn to computers, coding, and other technical fields due to their logical thinking and detail-oriented nature.

The Empathy Question: While some stereotypes portray autistic people as lacking empathy, this isn't always the case. They may express empathy differently, but many autistic people care deeply about others and can be incredibly loyal friends.

The Power of Potential: With early intervention and support, people with autism can thrive in all areas of life. They can develop fulfilling careers, build strong relationships, and make significant contributions to society.

Part 1: Understanding and Celebrating the Wonderful Autistic Brain
Chapter 3: Autism Facts and Anatomy :
3.2- The Neurological Basis of Autism (Brief overview)

Here's a brief overview of the neurological basis of Autism Spectrum Disorder (ASD):

The developing brain: Research suggests that autism involves differences in brain development, often occurring prenatally or in the first few years of life.

- **Brain connectivity:** Some studies indicate that atypical connections between brain regions might be present in autism. This could affect communication and information processing within the brain.

- **Brain function:** Certain areas of the brain, like those involved in social interaction, language processing, and sensory integration, may function differently in autistic individuals.

- **Genetics:** ASD has a strong genetic component, but it's complex and likely involves multiple genes interacting with environmental factors.

Important to Note:

- The exact neurological causes of autism are still being explored, and there's likely no single explanation.
- The way these factors manifest varies greatly, contributing to the spectrum nature of ASD.
- This is a brief overview, and further research is ongoing to understand the neurological underpinnings of autism.

Part 1: Understanding and Celebrating the Wonderful Autistic Brain
Chapter 4: Wonderful Things About Autism: Reframe challenges as strengths.

Here are some ways to reframe potential challenges associated with autism as strengths:

Challenge: Difficulty with social cues

- Strength: Literal thinker and honest communicator. People with autism often take things at face value, leading to clear and direct communication. This can be a valuable asset in situations requiring precise information or where hidden agendas can be a problem.

Challenge: Sensory processing differences

- Strength: Heightened sensory perception. Some autistic people experience the world in a more vivid way, with heightened sensitivity to sights, sounds, or textures. This can lead to a deeper appreciation for sensory details and a unique perspective on the environment.

Challenge: Repetitive behaviors and routines

- Strength: Detail-oriented and methodical. People with autism often thrive on structure and predictability. This strength allows them to excel at tasks requiring meticulous attention to detail and following established procedures.

Part 1: Understanding and Celebrating the Wonderful Autistic Brain
Chapter 4: Wonderful Things About Autism: Reframe challenges as strengths.

Challenge: Intense focus and passionate interests

- Strength: Subject-matter expertise and innovation. The intense focus of autistic individuals can lead to deep dives into specific topics, fostering expertise and the ability to identify unconventional solutions or hidden connections.

Challenge: Difficulty with social interaction

- Strength: Strong sense of self and unique perspective. People with autism may not always follow social norms, allowing them to develop their own unique identities and perspectives. This can be refreshing and lead to creative approaches in various fields.

Challenge: Preference for solitude

- Strength: Independent and self-sufficient. Autistic people who enjoy solitude may be highly resourceful and adept at working independently. This can be valuable in research, creative pursuits, or any field requiring focused work.

Challenge: Literal interpretation of language

- Strength: Clear and concise communication. Autistic people who take things literally may communicate in a straightforward and unambiguous manner. This can be crucial in technical fields or situations requiring precise language.

**Part 1: Understanding and Celebrating the Wonderful Autistic Brain
Chapter 4: Wonderful Things About Autism: Reframe challenges as strengths.**

Challenge: Difficulty understanding nonverbal communication

- Strength: Focus on the spoken word and clear communication. People with autism may rely heavily on verbal communication, leading them to excel at expressing themselves clearly and directly. This can be beneficial in situations requiring accurate information exchange.

Remember, these are just some examples, and the "wonderful things" about autism will vary from person to person. The key is to identify and celebrate the unique strengths that come with being autistic.

Part 2: Communication and Connection for Neurodiverse People

Chapter 5: Signs and Symptoms of Autism Spectrum Disorder (ASD)

Part 2: Communication and Connection for Neurodiverse People
Chapter 5: Signs and Symptoms of Autism Spectrum Disorder (ASD)

Autism Spectrum Disorder (ASD) affects how a person perceives and interacts with the world. Signs and symptoms can vary greatly, but here's a breakdown of some common areas to consider:

Social Communication and Interaction:

- Difficulties with nonverbal communication: This might include challenges understanding facial expressions, body language, or tone of voice.

- Trouble initiating or maintaining conversations: People with ASD may struggle taking turns, keeping a conversation flowing, or understanding social cues for when to speak.

- Limited social interests: They may prefer solitary activities or have very specific interests that they focus on intensely.

- Difficulty developing and maintaining relationships: Forming friendships and navigating social situations can be challenging.

Part 2: Communication and Connection for Neurodiverse People
Chapter 5: Signs and Symptoms of Autism Spectrum Disorder (ASD)

Restricted Interests and Repetitive Behaviors:

- Repetitive movements or behaviors: This could involve things like hand flapping, rocking, or lining objects up in a specific order.

- Inflexible routines: Sticking to routines and schedules can be very important, and changes can be upsetting.

- Fixated interests: Intense focus on specific topics or activities, often with in-depth knowledge accumulation.

- Sensory sensitivities: Some individuals may be oversensitive to certain sights, sounds, smells, tastes, or textures, while others may under-react to sensory input.

It's important to remember:

- These are just some common signs, and the way they manifest can vary greatly.

- Not everyone with ASD will experience all of these symptoms.

- The severity of symptoms can also vary significantly, contributing to the spectrum nature of ASD.

Part 2: Communication and Connection for Neurodiverse People
Chapter 5: Signs and Symptoms of Autism Spectrum Disorder (ASD)

Early Signs (by age 2):

- Little to no babbling or baby talk
- Limited eye contact
- Showing more interest in objects than people
- Not responding to their name or appearing not to hear you at times
- Playing with toys in an unusual or repetitive way

If you suspect someone you know may have ASD, it's crucial to seek a professional evaluation for a proper diagnosis. Early intervention can make a significant difference in a person's development and overall well-being.

Part 2: Communication and Connection for Neurodiverse People
Chapter 6: The Diagnostic Process for ASD: Early Intervention and Getting Help

The Diagnostic Process for ASD: Early Intervention and Getting Help

Diagnosing Autism Spectrum Disorder (ASD) involves a multi-disciplinary approach, typically led by a developmental pediatrician or child psychiatrist. Here's a breakdown of the process and the importance of early intervention:

The Evaluation:

- Comprehensive history: This involves gathering information from parents or caregivers about the child's development, behaviors, and any concerns.
- Developmental assessments: Standardized tests are used to assess the child's cognitive, language, social, and motor skills.
- Behavioral observations: Professionals will observe the child's interactions and behaviors during play or structured activities.
- Medical evaluation: A doctor may rule out other medical conditions that could be causing similar symptoms.

Early Intervention is Key:

- The earlier a diagnosis is received, the sooner interventions can begin.
- Early intervention can significantly improve a child's outcomes and future potential.
- It can help them develop essential skills in communication, social interaction, and managing challenging behaviors.

Part 2: Communication and Connection for Neurodiverse People
Chapter 6: The Diagnostic Process for ASD: Early Intervention and Getting Help

Getting Help:

- If your child receives an ASD diagnosis, there are various resources and support systems available:

- Early intervention programs: These programs provide specialized therapies and support to help children with ASD develop essential skills.

- Individualized Education Program (IEP): Schools can develop an IEP to provide your child with the necessary support and accommodations to succeed in school.

- Support groups: Connecting with other families who have children with ASD can be a valuable source of information and emotional support.

- Therapy services: Speech-language therapy, occupational therapy, and behavioral therapy can all be beneficial depending on the child's individual needs.

Remember:

A diagnosis of ASD is not a life sentence.
With the right support and interventions, people with ASD can thrive and live fulfilling lives.

Part 2: Communication and Connection for Neurodiverse People
Chapter 7: Understanding Nonverbal Communication for the Autistic Brain

Nonverbal communication, which includes facial expressions, body language, tone of voice, and gestures, can be a complex puzzle for the autistic brain. Here's a breakdown to help bridge the gap:

Challenges with Nonverbal Cues:

- Literal Interpretation: People with autism may take nonverbal cues literally, missing the underlying emotions or intentions. For example, a sarcastic tone might be misinterpreted as a serious statement.

- Difficulty Detecting Subtleties: Facial expressions can be fleeting, and autistic individuals may struggle to pick up on subtle changes in body language or tone.

- Information Overload: In social situations with multiple people, the sheer amount of nonverbal information can be overwhelming, making it difficult to process it all.

Part 2: Communication and Connection for Neurodiverse People
Chapter 6: The Diagnostic Process for ASD: Early Intervention and Getting Help

Strategies for Understanding Nonverbal Communication:

- Focus on the Basics: Start with clear, direct communication and avoid sarcasm or complex metaphors.

- Verbal Cues: Pair your words with clear facial expressions and gestures to emphasize your message.

- Explicit Communication: Don't rely solely on nonverbal cues. Explicitly state your feelings, needs, and intentions to avoid misunderstandings.

- Slow Down: Speak slowly and clearly, allowing processing time for the nonverbal cues you do provide.

- Visual Aids: Consider using pictures, social stories, or other visual tools to represent emotions and social situations.

- Practice Makes Progress: Role-playing different social scenarios can help build skills in interpreting nonverbal cues.

Part 2: Communication and Connection for Neurodiverse People
Chapter 6: The Diagnostic Process for ASD: Early Intervention and Getting Help

Things You Can Do to Help:

- Be Patient: It takes time and practice to develop these skills.

- Be Clear: Avoid vague instructions or expectations.

- Focus on Strengths: Some autistic individuals excel at written communication or interpreting specific nonverbal cues. Build on these strengths.

- Provide Context: Explain the social situation and the potential emotions involved to help them interpret nonverbal cues more accurately.

Additional Tips:

- Technology can help: There are apps and other tools available that can help translate facial expressions and body language into more readily understandable formats.
- Sensory Considerations: Be mindful of potential sensory sensitivities that might be affecting their ability to focus on nonverbal cues.

Remember: Communication is a two-way street. By adapting your communication style and providing support, you can create a more inclusive environment where everyone feels understood.

Part 3: Empowering Neurodiverse People: Social Skills, Emotional Management, and Self-Care

Chapter 8: The Importance of Social Skills and How They Develop

Part 3: Empowering Neurodiverse People: Social Skills, Emotional Management, and Self-Care

Chapter 8: The Importance of Social Skills and How They Develop

Social skills are the tools we use to interact and build relationships with others. They encompass a wide range of abilities, including:

- Communication: Verbal and nonverbal communication skills like active listening, expressing oneself clearly, and understanding different communication styles.

- Social awareness: Understanding social cues, norms, and expectations in different situations.

- Relationship building: Initiating friendships, maintaining connections, and showing empathy.

- Social problem-solving: Navigating conflict, resolving disagreements, and cooperating with others.

Part 3: Empowering Neurodiverse People: Social Skills, Emotional Management, and Self-Care
Chapter 8: The Importance of Social Skills and How They Develop

Why Are Social Skills Important?

Strong social skills are crucial for success in all aspects of life. They allow us to:

- Build and maintain healthy relationships: Strong social connections contribute to our emotional well-being and happiness.

- Succeed in school and work: Effective communication and collaboration are essential for academic and professional success.

- Navigate social situations: Social skills help us feel comfortable and confident in social settings.

- Develop empathy and understanding: By understanding others' perspectives, we can build stronger relationships.

Part 3: Empowering Neurodiverse People: Social Skills, Emotional Management, and Self-Care
Chapter 8: The Importance of Social Skills and How They Develop

How Do Social Skills Develop?

Social skills develop throughout childhood and adolescence through various experiences and interactions. Here are some key factors:

- Observation and Imitation: Children learn by observing and imitating the behavior of others, particularly parents, caregivers, and siblings.

- Direct Instruction: Parents and teachers can explicitly teach social skills by role-playing scenarios, providing feedback, and modeling appropriate behavior.

- Play: Social play with peers allows children to practice social interaction, cooperation, and conflict resolution.

- Social Experiences: Participating in various social activities like clubs, sports, or group projects provides opportunities to practice and develop social skills.

Part 3: Empowering Neurodiverse People: Social Skills, Emotional Management, and Self-Care
Chapter 8: The Importance of Social Skills and How They Develop

Social Skills Development in Autism:

Children with Autism Spectrum Disorder (ASD) may face challenges in developing social skills due to difficulties with communication, social awareness, and nonverbal cues. However, **with targeted interventions and support, they can learn and develop strong social skills. Here are some approaches that can be helpful:**

- Structured Social Skills Training: Programs that break down social skills into smaller steps and teach them in a structured way can be beneficial.

- Social Communication Groups: These groups provide opportunities for children to practice social interaction with peers in a safe and supportive environment.

- Visual Supports: Using visual aids like picture cards or social stories can help children understand social situations and expectations.

Remember:

Social skills development is a continuous process.
Early intervention is crucial for maximizing a child's potential. With patience, support, and the right strategies, everyone can develop strong social skills.

Part 3: Empowering Neurodiverse People: Social Skills, Emotional Management, and Self-Care
Chapter 9: Strategies for Developing Social Skills in Autistic People
9.1- strategies for developing social skills in autistic people:

Structured Learning:

- Social Skills Training Programs: These programs break down social skills into manageable steps, using techniques like role-playing, video modeling (watching others interact), and social scripts (predetermined responses for specific situations).

- Visual Supports: Utilize picture cards, social stories (narratives explaining social situations), and flowcharts to represent social interactions and expectations visually.

Supportive Environments:

- Social Communication Groups: These therapist-led groups provide a safe space for autistic individuals to practice social interaction with peers under guidance. Activities can focus on conversation starters, turn-taking, and group activities.

- Peer Support Groups: Connecting with other autistic people can provide a sense of belonging and allow them to learn from each other's experiences.

Part 3: Empowering Neurodiverse People: Social Skills, Emotional Management, and Self-Care

Chapter 9: Strategies for Developing Social Skills in Autistic People

9.1- strategies for developing social skills in autistic people:

Building Communication Skills:

- Direct Communication Training: Focus on clear and concise communication, avoiding sarcasm and metaphors that might be misinterpreted.

- Nonverbal Communication Cues: Practice identifying and understanding facial expressions, body language, and tone of voice. This can include using mirrors, video recordings, and emotion recognition apps.

- Technology Tools: Explore assistive communication devices or apps that can help with expressing needs, wants, and emotions.

Socialization Activities:

- Structured Playdates: Organize playdates with clear goals and activities. Start with short sessions and gradually increase duration as comfort levels improve.

- Shared Interests: Encourage participation in clubs, groups, or activities based on shared interests. This can provide a natural starting point for social interaction.

- Community Events: Attend age-appropriate social events or volunteer activities to practice social interaction in different settings.

Part 3: Empowering Neurodiverse People: Social Skills, Emotional Management, and Self-Care
Chapter 9: Strategies for Developing Social Skills in Autistic People
9.1- strategies for developing social skills in autistic people:

Additional Tips:

- Focus on Strengths: Build on existing strengths, like detailed observation skills, to enhance social interaction.

- Positive Reinforcement: Celebrate even small steps of progress and provide positive reinforcement to encourage continued effort.

- Individualized Approach: Tailor strategies to the specific needs and interests of the autistic person.

- Sensory Considerations: Be mindful of potential sensory sensitivities that might hinder their ability to focus on social interaction.

- Patience and Persistence: Developing social skills takes time and practice. Be patient and offer consistent support.

Remember:

- Social skills development is a journey, not a destination.

- Celebrate progress and focus on creating a supportive environment for growth.

- With the right strategies and encouragement, autistic people can develop strong social skills and build meaningful relationships.

Part 3: Empowering Neurodiverse People: Social Skills, Emotional Management, and Self-Care
Chapter 9: Strategies for Developing Social Skills in Autistic People
9.2- How the Autistic Brain Understands Social Cues

Hey there! We all know social stuff can be tricky, but for the autistic brain, it can sometimes feel like a whole different language. Here's the inside scoop on how your brain might be processing social cues differently, and some tips to help bridge the gap.

The Challenge:

Imagine the world as a giant information overload. Your brain is awesome at picking up on all the details – sights, sounds, even the tiniest changes in the air. But sometimes, this can make it hard to focus on the social stuff, like that raised eyebrow your friend just gave you.

Here's what might be happening:

- Literal Thinkers: You might take things very literally, missing the hidden messages behind facial expressions or jokes. Like, if someone says "That was a breeze," you might not realize they're saying something was easy.

- Movie Magic vs. Reality: Social cues in movies and TV shows can be exaggerated, making real-life interactions seem confusing. A smile on TV might mean happiness, but in real life, it could be nervousness or just being polite.

Part 3: Empowering Neurodiverse People: Social Skills, Emotional Management, and Self-Care
Chapter 9: Strategies for Developing Social Skills in Autistic People
9.2- How the Autistic Brain Understands Social Cues

Information Overload: In a crowded room, there's just so much going on! All the sounds, smells, and sights can make it hard to pay attention to what people are saying and how they're saying it.

Cracking the Code:

Don't worry, there are ways to understand the social world better! Here are some tips:

- Focus on the Basics: People use facial expressions, body language, and tone of voice to communicate, but sometimes it's subtle. Start by focusing on the main message someone is trying to say with their words.

- Ask for Clarification: If something seems confusing, don't be afraid to ask! A simple "What do you mean by that?" can clear things up and avoid misunderstandings.

- Superpower Alert! Your amazing attention to detail can be a social strength. Notice patterns in how people act and what certain things might mean.

Part 3: Empowering Neurodiverse People: Social Skills, Emotional Management, and Self-Care
Chapter 9: Strategies for Developing Social Skills in Autistic People
9.2- How the Autistic Brain Understands Social Cues

Making Connections:

Socializing can be fun, but it can also be tiring. Here are some ways to make things a little easier:

- Find Your Tribe: Look for people who share your interests! Talking about things you love can make social interaction more natural and enjoyable.

- Start Small: Don't try to tackle huge parties right away. Begin with shorter interactions, like one-on-one conversations or small group activities.

- Take Breaks: Social situations can be draining. If you need a break, step outside, listen to music for a few minutes, or find a quiet corner to recharge.

Remember: You're not alone! Many people have challenges with social cues, and the autistic brain has unique strengths that can be amazing assets in social situations. With a little practice and these tips, you can navigate the social world with confidence!

Part 3: Empowering Neurodiverse People: Social Skills, Emotional Management, and Self-Care
Chapter 10: Managing Feelings in the Autistic Brain: Emotional Regulation Strategies

The autistic brain is amazing at processing information, but sometimes emotions can feel like a rollercoaster ride. Here are some strategies to help you manage those feelings and stay in control:

Understanding Your Triggers:

The first step is figuring out what sets you off. Maybe it's loud noises, crowded places, or unexpected changes in routine. Once you know your triggers, you can develop a plan to deal with them.

Sensory Overload SOS:

Sometimes, the world just gets too much! Here are some ideas to calm your senses:

- Visual: Ditch the bright lights! Dim the lights, wear sunglasses, or find a quiet corner.

- Auditory: Block out the noise! Use earplugs, noise-canceling headphones, or listen to calming music.

- Tactile: Find a calming texture. Fidget with a stress ball, hug a soft pillow, or wear comfortable clothes.

Part 3: Empowering Neurodiverse People: Social Skills, Emotional Management, and Self-Care
Chapter 10: Managing Feelings in the Autistic Brain: Emotional Regulation Strategies

Calming Techniques Toolbox:

Everyone has their own way of chilling out. Here are some ideas to experiment with and find what works for you:

- Deep Breathing: Take slow, deep breaths in through your nose and out through your mouth. Imagine you're blowing out birthday candles.

- Mindfulness: Focus on the present moment. Notice your surroundings and how your body feels. There are many mindfulness apps and exercises available online.

- Stimming: Repetitive movements like rocking, flapping your hands, or tapping your foot can be calming for some people. Just make sure it's not disruptive to others.

- Weighted Vest: The gentle pressure of a weighted vest can feel comforting and grounding.

Part 3: Empowering Neurodiverse People: Social Skills, Emotional Management, and Self-Care
Chapter 10: Managing Feelings in the Autistic Brain: Emotional Regulation Strategies

Communicate Your Needs:

Letting people know what you need can be super helpful. Here are some ways to do it:

- The "I Feel" Statement: "I feel overwhelmed when it gets too loud. Can we take a break?"

- Visual Cues: Use pictures or symbols to communicate your needs, like a noise-cancelling headphone symbol for needing quiet time.

- Talk to a Trusted Person: Tell a friend, family member, or therapist about your challenges and how they can support you.

Remember:

- It's okay to not be okay. Everyone experiences strong emotions sometimes.
- There's no one-size-fits-all solution. Experiment and find what works best for you.
- Be patient with yourself. Learning to manage emotions takes time and practice.
- Bonus Tip: Celebrate your victories! Even small steps towards managing your emotions are a win. Reward yourself for your progress!

Part 3: Empowering Neurodiverse People: Social Skills, Emotional Management, and Self-Care
Chapter 11: Physical Self-Care for Autistic People
11.1- Movement and Sensory Regulation

The autistic brain often processes sensory information differently. This can sometimes lead to feeling overwhelmed or out of sync. Movement can be a powerful tool for regulating your senses and finding a sense of calm. Here's how:

The Body Connection:

- Movement and the Nervous System: Physical activity helps regulate the nervous system, which can calm feelings of anxiety or overwhelm.

- Sensory Input and Output: Movement can provide a healthy outlet for sensory input. Engaging your body can help you process and organize sensory information more effectively.

Movement Strategies:

- Proprioception Power: Activities that provide deep pressure and joint stimulation can be very calming. This might include things like:

- Weighted vests: The gentle pressure can feel grounding and comforting.

- Joint compressions: Deep squeezes or hugs can provide a sense of security.

Part 3: Empowering Neurodiverse People: Social Skills, Emotional Management, and Self-Care
Chapter 11: Physical Self-Care for Autistic People
11.1- Movement and Sensory Regulation

- Heavy work: Activities like pushing a weighted object or carrying groceries can be helpful.

- Vestibular Fun: Movement that stimulates the balance system can be calming or alerting, depending on your needs. Try:

- Rocking: Back-and-forth rocking on a chair or swing can be very soothing.

- Spinning: Spin slowly in a safe environment (like a swivel chair) if you find it calming.

- Jumping: Jumping on a trampoline or jumping on the bed (with adult supervision) can be a great way to release energy.

- Rhythmic Movements: Repetitive movements can be calming and focusing. Explore:

- Pacing: Walking back and forth in a designated space can help some people regulate their emotions.

- Dancing: Move your body to the music! Dancing is a fun way to express yourself and get exercise.

- Stimming: If repetitive movements like hand flapping or tapping are self-soothing, find ways to do them discreetly if needed.

Part 3: Empowering Neurodiverse People: Social Skills, Emotional Management, and Self-Care
Chapter 11: Physical Self-Care for Autistic People
11.1- Movement and Sensory Regulation

Finding Your Groove:

- Experiment and explore: There's no one-size-fits-all approach. Try different types of movement and see what works best for you.

- Listen to your body: Pay attention to how different movements make you feel. Choose activities that promote calmness and focus.

- Incorporate movement into your routine: Schedule short movement breaks throughout the day to help manage sensory input and stay regulated.

- Movement can be a powerful tool for managing sensory sensitivities and promoting a sense of well-being. Find what works for you and embrace the power of movement!

Part 3: Empowering Neurodiverse People: Social Skills, Emotional Management, and Self-Care
Chapter 11: Physical Self-Care for Autistic People
11.2- Stimulating the Vagus Nerve for Calming and Focus

The vagus nerve has become a bit of a hot topic lately, and for good reason! It's the main nerve of the parasympathetic nervous system, which is responsible for our body's "rest and digest" response. When stimulated, the vagus nerve can help us relax, focus, and feel calmer. Here's how it relates to autism and some things to consider:

The Vagus Nerve and Autism:

While research is ongoing, some studies suggest that the vagus nerve function might be different in people with autism. This could contribute to challenges with relaxation and focus. However, stimulating the vagus nerve may offer some potential benefits.

Stimulating the Vagus Nerve:

There are several ways to stimulate the vagus nerve, although some have stronger scientific backing than others. Here are a few options:

- Deep Breathing Exercises: Slow, deep breaths activate the vagus nerve, promoting relaxation and focus. Try inhaling for a count of four, holding for a count of seven, and exhaling for a count of eight.

- Humming or Singing: Chanting or humming stimulates the vagus nerve through vibrations in the throat.

Part 3: Empowering Neurodiverse People: Social Skills, Emotional Management, and Self-Care
Chapter 11: Physical Self-Care for Autistic People
11.2- Stimulating the Vagus Nerve for Calming and Focus

- Cold Exposure: Short bursts of cold exposure, like a cold shower or splashing cold water on your face, can activate the vagus nerve. Be sure to start slow and listen to your body's tolerance. (Important: Consult a doctor before trying cold exposure if you have any underlying health conditions.)

Other Techniques:

Some techniques with less scientific evidence, but anecdotal reports of effectiveness, include:

- Acupressure: Applying pressure to specific points on the body is thought to stimulate the vagus nerve.

- Massage: Massage therapy can activate the vagus nerve and promote relaxation.

Part 3: Empowering Neurodiverse People: Social Skills, Emotional Management, and Self-Care
Chapter 11: Physical Self-Care for Autistic People
11.2- Stimulating the Vagus Nerve for Calming and Focus

Important Considerations:

- Talk to your doctor: Before trying any new technique, especially cold exposure or acupressure, consult your doctor to ensure it's safe for you.

- Focus on healthy habits: While vagus nerve stimulation can be helpful, it's not a magic bullet. Maintaining a healthy lifestyle with regular exercise, good sleep, and a balanced diet is crucial for overall well-being.

- Individualized approach: What works for one person might not work for another. Experiment and find what techniques promote relaxation and focus for you.

- Overall, stimulating the vagus nerve shows promise as a way to promote calmness and focus. While more research is needed, incorporating some of these techniques into your daily routine might be a helpful addition to your self-care toolbox.

Part 3: Empowering Neurodiverse People: Social Skills, Emotional Management, and Self-Care
Chapter 12: Healthy Nutrition for Autistic People
12.1- Creating a Balanced Diet

While there's no single "autism diet," focusing on a balanced and nutritious approach can significantly benefit autistic individuals. This builds upon the foundation of a healthy diet for everyone, but also considers some unique aspects that can impact autistic people's eating habits.

Addressing Sensory Sensitivities:

- Texture: Some autistic individuals have sensitivities to certain textures. Explore different ways to prepare foods – pureeing, chopping into smaller pieces, or offering a variety of textures within a meal can be helpful.

- Taste: Strong flavors or overwhelming sweetness can be off-putting. Experiment with herbs and spices to add subtle flavors, and offer blander options alongside more flavorful ones.

- Smell: Certain smells might be overpowering. Allow for individual preferences and be mindful of strong-smelling foods during mealtimes.

Part 3: Empowering Neurodiverse People: Social Skills, Emotional Management, and Self-Care
Chapter 12: Healthy Nutrition for Autistic People
12.1- Creating a Balanced Diet

Considering Selective Eating:

- Limited Food Preferences: Many autistic people have restricted food preferences. Offer a variety of options within their preferred categories and gradually introduce new foods alongside familiar ones.

- Routine and Predictability: Sticking to a routine can be comforting. Create a meal plan with some flexibility, allowing for occasional choices or substitutions within familiar food groups.

- Positive Reinforcement: Focus on praise and encouragement during mealtimes. Avoid pressuring or forcing someone to eat something they dislike.

Part 3: Empowering Neurodiverse People: Social Skills, Emotional Management, and Self-Care
Chapter 12: Healthy Nutrition for Autistic People
12.1- Creating a Balanced Diet

Building a Balanced Plate:

Just like for everyone else, a balanced diet is crucial for autistic individuals. Here's how we can adapt the core principles:

- Fruits and Vegetables: Offer a variety of colors, textures, and preparations to cater to sensory preferences. Frozen fruits can be a good option, and smoothies can be a fun way to incorporate fruits and vegetables.

- Whole Grains: Whole-wheat bread, brown rice, quinoa, and whole-wheat pasta provide sustained energy. Experiment with different grain options to find textures that are enjoyable.

- Lean Protein: Baked fish, chicken, beans, lentils, tofu, and nuts are all excellent sources of lean protein. Again, consider texture preferences and offer choices.

- Healthy Fats: Include healthy fats like avocado, olive oil, nuts, and fatty fish in moderation. Experiment with incorporating them into favorite dishes.

Part 3: Empowering Neurodiverse People: Social Skills, Emotional Management, and Self-Care
Chapter 12: Healthy Nutrition for Autistic People
12.1- Creating a Balanced Diet

Additional Considerations:

- Gut Health: A healthy gut microbiome is essential for overall health and may be particularly important for some autistic individuals. Consider incorporating gut-friendly foods like yogurt (with live cultures), kimchi, and sauerkraut (if tolerated).

- Dietary Consultations: A registered dietitian familiar with autism spectrum disorder (ASD) can provide personalized guidance and support in creating a balanced meal plan that caters to individual needs and preferences.

Remember:

- Focus on the Whole Person: Consider sensory sensitivities, dietary preferences, and overall well-being when creating a meal plan.

- Make it a Collaborative Effort: Involving autistic individuals in meal planning and preparation, whenever possible, can promote a sense of ownership and encourage positive mealtime experiences.

- Celebrate Small Victories: Progress can be gradual. Celebrate even small victories, like trying a new texture or incorporating a new healthy option into a favorite dish.

Part 3: Empowering Neurodiverse People: Social Skills, Emotional Management, and Self-Care
Chapter 12: Healthy Nutrition for Autistic People
12.1- Creating a Balanced Diet

By creating a balanced and sensory-friendly approach to nutrition, we can empower autistic individuals to develop healthy eating habits and experience the positive impact of good nutrition on their overall health and well-being. This builds upon the general principles of a balanced diet, but acknowledges the unique needs and preferences of autistic people.

Part 3: Empowering Neurodiverse People: Social Skills, Emotional Management, and Self-Care
Chapter 12: Healthy Nutrition for Autistic People
12.2- Essential Vitamins and Minerals

There isn't enough evidence to show that specific vitamins or minerals can cure or treat autism spectrum disorder (ASD). However, some research suggests that deficiencies in certain vitamins and minerals may be more common in autistic children than in neurotypical children. Here are some essential vitamins and minerals that may be of interest:

Vitamin D

- Vitamin D is important for bone health and the immune system. Some studies suggest that children with autism may have lower levels of vitamin D.

- Getting enough sunlight can help your body produce vitamin D. Fatty fish, egg yolks, and fortified foods are also good sources of vitamin D.

Magnesium

- Magnesium is a mineral that is involved in many bodily functions, including muscle and nerve function. Some studies suggest that children with autism may have lower levels of magnesium.

- Leafy green vegetables, nuts, seeds, and whole grains are all good sources of magnesium.

Part 3: Empowering Neurodiverse People: Social Skills, Emotional Management, and Self-Care
Chapter 12: Healthy Nutrition for Autistic People
12.2- Essential Vitamins and Minerals

Vitamin B6

- Vitamin B6 is important for brain function and development. Some studies suggest that vitamin B6 supplements may improve some symptoms of autism, such as irritability and hyperactivity.

- Chicken, fish, beans, potatoes, and bananas are all good sources of vitamin B6.

Omega3 fatty acids

- Omega-3 fatty acids are important for brain development and function. Some studies suggest that omega-3 fatty acids supplements may improve some symptoms of autism, such as social interaction and communication.

- Fatty fish, such as salmon, tuna, and mackerel, are good sources of omega-3 fatty acids.

If you are concerned that your child may have a vitamin or mineral deficiency, talk to their doctor. They can test your child's blood levels and recommend a supplement if needed. It is important to note that high doses of some vitamins and minerals can be toxic, so it is important to only take supplements under the supervision of a doctor.

Part 3: Empowering Neurodiverse People: Social Skills, Emotional Management, and Self-Care
Chapter 12: Healthy Nutrition for Autistic People
12.3- The Importance of Omega-3s, Magnesium, and Vitamin B6

While there's no cure for Autism Spectrum Disorder (ASD), some research suggests that Omega-3s, magnesium, and Vitamin B6 may play a role in managing certain symptoms. Here's a breakdown of their potential importance:

Omega-3 Fatty Acids:

- Brain Health: Omega-3s are crucial for brain development and function. Some studies suggest they may improve communication, social interaction, and repetitive behaviors in autistic individuals.

- Sources: Fatty fish (salmon, tuna, mackerel), flaxseeds, walnuts, and chia seeds are rich in Omega-3s.

Magnesium:

- Neurological Function: Magnesium plays a role in nerve transmission and muscle function. Studies suggest deficiencies might be linked to anxiety, hyperactivity, and sleep problems, common in ASD.

- Sources: Leafy green vegetables, nuts, seeds, whole grains, and legumes are good sources of magnesium.

Part 3: Empowering Neurodiverse People: Social Skills, Emotional Management, and Self-Care
Chapter 12: Healthy Nutrition for Autistic People
12.3- The Importance of Omega-3s, Magnesium, and Vitamin B6

Vitamin B6:

- Brain Development: Vitamin B6 is essential for brain function and development. Some studies suggest it may improve irritability and hyperactivity in autistic individuals.
- Sources: Chicken, fish, beans, potatoes, and bananas are good sources of Vitamin B6.

Important Considerations:

- Research is ongoing: While these nutrients show promise, more research is needed to confirm their definitive role in managing ASD symptoms.

- Individualized Needs: The impact of these nutrients can vary greatly between individuals. Consulting a doctor or registered dietitian is crucial to determine if supplementation is necessary.

- Food First: Aim to get these nutrients through dietary sources whenever possible. Supplements should be considered alongside a healthy diet and not as a replacement.

Part 3: Empowering Neurodiverse People: Social Skills, Emotional Management, and Self-Care
Chapter 12: Healthy Nutrition for Autistic People
12.3- The Importance of Omega-3s, Magnesium, and Vitamin B6

Remember:

- A balanced diet and healthy lifestyle habits are essential for everyone, including those with ASD.

- If you're considering supplements, consult a doctor to ensure proper dosage and avoid potential interactions with medications.

- These nutrients might be part of a comprehensive approach to managing ASD symptoms, but they are not a cure.

Part 3: Empowering Neurodiverse People: Social Skills, Emotional Management, and Self-Care
Chapter 12: Healthy Nutrition for Autistic People
12.4- Dietary Sources of Protein, Fiber, and Calcium

Here's a breakdown of delicious dietary sources rich in protein, fiber, and calcium:

Protein Powerhouses:

- Animal Sources: Lean meats (chicken, turkey, fish), eggs, dairy products (milk, yogurt, cheese) are all excellent sources of complete protein, containing all essential amino acids your body needs.

- Plant-Based Options: Beans, lentils, tofu, tempeh, nuts, and seeds are great protein sources for vegetarians and vegans. While some plant-based proteins are incomplete (lacking one or more essential amino acids), you can combine different plant proteins throughout the day to create complete protein sources. For example, rice and beans is a classic complete protein combination.

Fiber Fantastic Foods:

- Fruits and Vegetables: Most fruits and vegetables contain fiber, with higher concentrations in the skin and inedible seeds. Think berries, apples with skin, pears with skin, leafy greens, broccoli, and sweet potatoes.

- Whole Grains: Opt for whole grains over refined grains whenever possible. Whole grains like brown rice, quinoa, oats, whole-wheat bread, and whole-wheat pasta are packed with fiber.

Part 3: Empowering Neurodiverse People: Social Skills, Emotional Management, and Self-Care
Chapter 12: Healthy Nutrition for Autistic People
12.4- Dietary Sources of Protein, Fiber, and Calcium

Beans and Legumes: Beans, lentils, and peas are triple threats, offering protein, fiber, and some even contain calcium!

Calcium Champions:

- Dairy Delights: Dairy products like milk, yogurt, and cheese are classic sources of calcium. Choose low-fat or fat-free options to keep saturated fat intake in check.

- Leafy Green Power: Don't underestimate the power of veggies! Dark leafy greens like kale, collard greens, and Swiss chard are surprisingly good sources of calcium.

- Fortified Foods: Some plant-based milks, cereals, and orange juice are fortified with calcium, making them good options for those who consume limited dairy products. Be sure to check the label to ensure the calcium fortification.

- Seafood Options: Canned sardines and salmon (with bones) are excellent sources of calcium. Just be mindful of portion sizes due to mercury content in some fish.

- Seeds: Sesame seeds, chia seeds, and poppy seeds are all good sources of calcium, although they need to be consumed in larger quantities to meet daily recommendations compared to dairy products.

Part 3: Empowering Neurodiverse People: Social Skills, Emotional Management, and Self-Care
Chapter 12: Healthy Nutrition for Autistic People
12.4- Dietary Sources of Protein, Fiber, and Calcium

Remember:

Aim for a balanced diet that incorporates a variety of these foods throughout the day to ensure you're getting enough protein, fiber, and calcium.

Consult a registered dietitian for personalized dietary advice tailored to your specific needs and preferences.

Part 4: Expanding Language Skills in the Autistic Brain

Chapter 13: Strategies to Enhance Language Skills

Part 4: Expanding Language Skills in the Autistic Brain
Chapter 13: Strategies to Enhance Language Skills

Here are some strategies to enhance language skills, applicable to both children and adults:

Exposure and Input:

- Reading: Reading exposes you to new vocabulary, grammar structures, and proper sentence construction. Read books, articles, blogs, or anything that interests you.

- Listening: Immerse yourself in spoken language. Listen to audiobooks, podcasts, educational videos, or music with meaningful lyrics. Pay attention to pronunciation and how language flows in conversation.

- Conversations: Engage in conversations with others! Talk to friends, family, or join groups or clubs that center around your interests. This provides opportunities to practice using language in a real-world setting.

Active Learning:

- Vocabulary Building: Make a conscious effort to learn new words every day. Use flashcards, apps, or keep a vocabulary notebook.

- Grammar Practice: Brush up on grammar basics through online exercises, workbooks, or grammar websites.

- Interactive Activities: Learning can be fun! Play word games, do crossword puzzles, or participate in online language learning platforms that offer interactive exercises.

Part 4: Expanding Language Skills in the Autistic Brain
Chapter 13: Strategies to Enhance Language Skills

Output and Practice:

- Writing: Writing allows you to organize your thoughts and practice using language in a structured way. Start a journal, write short stories, or create a blog.

- Speaking Opportunities: Don't be afraid to speak up! Volunteer for presentations, join a debate club, or find opportunities to practice public speaking.

- Shadowing: Listen to a short audio clip and then repeat what you hear, mimicking the pronunciation and intonation as closely as possible. This can help improve fluency and speaking style.

Additional Tips:

- Find a Language Partner: Connect with someone who is a native speaker of the language you're learning or someone who wants to improve their skills in the same language you do. You can practice conversation and help each other learn.

- Make it Relevant: Focus on learning language related to your interests or hobbies. This will make the learning process more engaging and enjoyable.

- Celebrate Progress: Learning a language takes time and effort. Acknowledge your improvements and celebrate your milestones to stay motivated.

Part 4: Expanding Language Skills in the Autistic Brain
Chapter 13: Strategies to Enhance Language Skills

- Don't be Afraid to Make Mistakes: Everyone makes mistakes when learning a new language. Embrace them as learning opportunities and keep practicing.

Remember:

- Consistency is key! Dedicate some time each day, even if it's just for a short period, to practice and improve your language skills.

- There's no one-size-fits-all approach. Find strategies that work best for you and make learning enjoyable.

- With dedication and consistent effort, you can significantly enhance your language skills and communication abilities.

Part 4: Expanding Language Skills in the Autistic Brain
Chapter 14: Understanding Language Processing in the Autistic Brain:

Language processing can be a complex puzzle, and sometimes there can be roadblocks that make understanding and using language difficult. Here are some potential challenges to consider:

- Auditory Processing Difficulties (APD): People with APD may have trouble distinguishing sounds, especially in noisy environments. This can make it hard to follow conversations, understand fast speech, or pick up on subtle cues like sarcasm or changes in tone.

- Literal Interpretations: Some individuals might take everything very literally, missing the implied meaning behind figurative language like idioms (expressions with non-literal meanings) or jokes. For example, the phrase "It's raining cats and dogs" might be interpreted as a literal downpour of furry animals.

- Difficulties with Sequencing: Organizing thoughts and ideas into a coherent sequence can be challenging. This can make it difficult to follow a conversation thread, tell stories in a clear order, or write grammatically correct sentences.

- Working Memory Issues: Holding information in your mind for short periods can be difficult. This can make it hard to follow multi-step instructions, understand complex sentences, or remember the context of a conversation.

Part 4: Expanding Language Skills in the Autistic Brain
Chapter 14: Understanding Language Processing in the Autistic Brain:

- Sensory Sensitivities: Background noise, strong smells, or bright lights can be overwhelming and distracting, making it difficult to focus on processing language.

These challenges can affect people in different ways and to varying degrees. Here's how they might manifest in communication:

- Misunderstandings: Difficulty processing spoken language can lead to misunderstandings and frustration.

- Social Anxiety: Fear of misinterpreting social cues or struggling to follow conversations can lead to social anxiety and withdrawal.

- Limited Vocabulary: Difficulties with auditory processing or memory can make it hard to learn and retain new words, limiting vocabulary development.

- Difficulties Expressing Oneself: Challenges with organizing thoughts or forming sentences can make it difficult to express oneself clearly and effectively.

Part 4: Expanding Language Skills in the Autistic Brain
Chapter 14: Understanding Language Processing in the Autistic Brain:

Remember:

- These challenges are not a reflection of intelligence. People with language processing difficulties can be just as intelligent and capable as anyone else.

- There are strategies and tools available to help! Speech therapy, assistive listening devices, and visual supports can make a big difference.

- With the right support and understanding, people with language processing difficulties can learn to communicate effectively and confidently.

Part 4: Expanding Language Skills in the Autistic Brain
Chapter 14: Understanding Language Processing in the Autistic Brain:

14.1- Explain different learning styles that may be present in autistic individuals.

The beauty of the autistic brain is its diversity! Just like everyone else, autistic individuals learn in different ways. Here's a breakdown of some common learning styles you might encounter:

Visual Learners:

- Strengths: Thrive on visual information like pictures, diagrams, charts, written instructions, and social stories (narratives explaining social situations).

- Learning Strategies: Utilize visual aids, flashcards, graphic organizers, mind maps, and high-contrast text.

Auditory Learners:

- Strengths: Learn best by listening to instructions, lectures, audiobooks, or songs.

- Learning Strategies: Record lectures or instructions, use audiobooks, and encourage repetition through rhymes or songs.

Part 4: Expanding Language Skills in the Autistic Brain
Chapter 14: Understanding Language Processing in the Autistic Brain:

14.1- Explain different learning styles that may be present in autistic individuals.

Kinesthetic Learners (Hands-on Learners):

- Strengths: Grasp concepts best through movement and physical activity.

- Learning Strategies: Incorporate movement into learning, like role-playing social situations, using manipulatives (objects for hands-on learning), or acting out stories.

Social Learners:

- Strengths: Learn best through interaction and collaboration with others.

- Learning Strategies: Facilitate group projects, peer tutoring, or social learning activities.

Remember:

- Combinations are common: Many autistic individuals have a combination of learning styles.

- Individualized approach is key: The most effective learning strategies will vary depending on the person. Observe and identify what works best for the individual.

- Strengths-based approach: Build on existing strengths and preferences to enhance learning and motivation.

Part 4: Expanding Language Skills in the Autistic Brain
Chapter 14: Understanding Language Processing in the Autistic Brain:

14.1- Explain different learning styles that may be present in autistic individuals.

Here are some additional considerations for autistic learners:

- Sensory Sensitivities: Bright lights, loud noises, or certain textures can be distracting or overwhelming. Create a sensory-friendly learning environment to minimize distractions.

- Literal Interpretations: Be clear, concise, and avoid sarcasm or figurative language.

- Provide Clear Expectations: Use routines, visual schedules, and social stories to help autistic learners understand what is expected of them.

- Allow for Breaks: Schedule short breaks throughout learning activities to avoid overwhelm.

By understanding different learning styles and addressing potential challenges, we can create a more inclusive learning environment where everyone can thrive.

Part 4: Expanding Language Skills in the Autistic Brain
Chapter 15: Building a Strong Foundation for Language Development:
15.1- Focus on early intervention strategies for children with ASD.

Early intervention is crucial for children with Autism Spectrum Disorder (ASD) as their brains are highly receptive to learning and development during this time. Here are some key strategies for early intervention:

1. Comprehensive Evaluation:

A thorough assessment by a qualified professional (pediatrician, psychologist, etc.) is vital to determine the child's strengths, weaknesses, and specific needs. This will guide the development of an individualized intervention plan.

2. Applied Behavior Analysis (ABA):

ABA is a widely recognized evidence-based therapy that focuses on breaking down skills into smaller, achievable steps. Through positive reinforcement and consistent practice, children learn desired behaviors and communication skills.

3. Speech Therapy:

Speech therapy can address a variety of challenges, including language delays, articulation difficulties, and social communication skills. Therapists work on vocabulary development, using appropriate sentence structures, and understanding nonverbal cues.

Part 4: Expanding Language Skills in the Autistic Brain
Chapter 15: Building a Strong Foundation for Language Development:
15.1- Focus on early intervention strategies for children with ASD.

4. Social Skills Training:

Explicitly teaching social skills can be very beneficial. Therapists may use role-playing activities, social stories, and group activities to help children understand social cues, initiate interactions, and build relationships with peers.

5. Occupational Therapy:

Occupational therapists can help with sensory processing difficulties, motor skills development, and self-care tasks. They may use sensory integration techniques, fine motor activities, and functional play experiences to address these challenges.

6. Parent Training:

Parents and caregivers play a vital role in a child's development. Training programs equip them with strategies to implement intervention techniques at home, ensuring consistency and maximizing progress.

7. Play-Based Therapy:

Play is a natural way for children to learn and explore. Therapists may use structured or unstructured play to encourage social interaction, communication, and emotional expression.

Part 4: Expanding Language Skills in the Autistic Brain
Chapter 15: Building a Strong Foundation for Language Development:
15.1- Focus on early intervention strategies for children with ASD.

8. Visual Supports:

Visual aids like picture cards, schedules, and social stories can be incredibly helpful for autistic children who often process information visually. They provide structure, clarity, and predictability, reducing anxiety and promoting understanding.

9. Sensory Integration Techniques:

Some children with ASD may have sensory sensitivities or processing difficulties. Therapists can use techniques like sensory diets (planned activities to address sensory needs) or calming strategies to help them manage their sensory experiences.

10. Family Support:

Having a child with ASD can be challenging for families. Support groups, parent training programs, and access to resources can help families cope with the demands and navigate the journey.

Part 4: Expanding Language Skills in the Autistic Brain
Chapter 15: Building a Strong Foundation for Language Development:
15.1- Focus on early intervention strategies for children with ASD.

Remember:

- Early intervention is most effective when started as soon as possible.

- The specific strategies used will vary depending on the child's individual needs and developmental level.

- Consistency and collaboration between therapists, parents, and educators are vital for a child's success.

- Early intervention can significantly improve a child's outcomes and set them on a path for a fulfilling life.

Additional Resources:

- Centers for Disease Control and Prevention (CDC): https://www.cdc.gov/autism/index.html
- National Institute of Child Health and Human Development (NICHD): https://www.nichd.nih.gov/health/topics/autism
- Autism Speaks: https://www.autismspeaks.org/

Part 4: Expanding Language Skills in the Autistic Brain
Chapter 15: Building a Strong Foundation for Language Development:
15.2- Discuss the importance of receptive language skills and how to develop them.

Receptive language skills are the foundation for communication and understanding the world around us. They encompass everything we do to take in and process spoken or written language. Here's why they're so important and how to develop them:

The Power of Understanding:

- Learning and Development: Strong receptive language skills are crucial for learning new things. By understanding instructions, explanations, and stories, children can build knowledge and develop cognitive skills.

- Social Interaction: Understanding language is key to following conversations, responding appropriately, and building relationships. It allows us to participate in discussions, ask questions, and share our thoughts and feelings.

- Emotional Well-being: Being able to understand what others are saying can help us feel connected, avoid misunderstandings, and navigate social situations more confidently.

Part 4: Expanding Language Skills in the Autistic Brain
Chapter 15: Building a Strong Foundation for Language Development:
15.2- Discuss the importance of receptive language skills and how to develop them.

Building Strong Receptive Skills:

Here are some strategies to help children (and adults!) develop strong receptive language skills:

- Exposure and Input: Immerse yourself in language! Read books, listen to audiobooks, watch educational shows (with captions if needed), and engage in conversations. The more you're exposed to language, the better you'll understand it.

- Interactive Activities: Learning is fun! Play games that involve listening and following instructions, like Simon Says or I Spy. Engage in storytelling activities, where you take turns adding to a story.

- Clear Communication: Speak clearly and concisely, using simple language and avoiding complex sentence structures when first introducing new concepts.

- Visual Aids: Visuals can be powerful tools for understanding. Use pictures, flashcards, gestures, and facial expressions to support spoken language.

- Repetition and Practice: Repetition is key to learning. Repeat instructions, rephrase sentences if needed, and provide opportunities for practice.

Part 4: Expanding Language Skills in the Autistic Brain
Chapter 15: Building a Strong Foundation for Language Development:
15.2- Discuss the importance of receptive language skills and how to develop them.

- Active Listening: Encourage active listening by asking questions, making eye contact, and summarizing what you've heard.

Additional Tips:

- Tailor your approach: Consider the individual's age, interests, and learning style when choosing activities.
- Make it fun and engaging: Learning should be enjoyable! Choose activities that spark interest and keep the learner motivated.

- Celebrate progress: Acknowledge and celebrate improvements, no matter how small. Positive reinforcement keeps learners motivated.

- Seek professional help: If you have concerns about a child's receptive language development, consult a speech-language pathologist for an evaluation and personalized strategies.

Remember:

Developing strong receptive language skills takes time and consistent effort. By creating a stimulating and supportive environment, we can help children (and adults!) unlock the power of understanding and communication.

Part 4: Expanding Language Skills in the Autistic Brain
Chapter 15: Building a Strong Foundation for Language Development:
15.3- Cover foundational skills like building vocabulary, using simple sentence structures, and improving communication clarity.

Communication is a cornerstone of human connection. It allows us to share ideas, build relationships, and navigate the world around us. But strong communication starts with a solid foundation – vocabulary, sentence structure, and clarity. Here's how to strengthen these foundational skills:

1. Building a Rich Vocabulary:

- Exposure is Key: Read books, articles, and listen to podcasts on a variety of topics. The more you encounter new words, the more likely you are to understand and use them.

- Active Learning: Don't just passively consume content. Look up unfamiliar words in a dictionary or online, and actively try to incorporate them into your conversations or writing.

- Make it Fun: Play word games like Scrabble or Boggle, do crossword puzzles, or create vocabulary flashcards with pictures or definitions.

- Use it or Lose it: Once you learn a new word, try to use it in conversation or writing as soon as possible. This helps solidify it in your memory.

Part 4: Expanding Language Skills in the Autistic Brain
Chapter 15: Building a Strong Foundation for Language Development:
15.3- Cover foundational skills like building vocabulary, using simple sentence structures, and improving communication clarity.

2. Mastering Simple Sentence Structures:

- Subject-Verb-Object: Start with the basics. Focus on constructing clear sentences with a subject (who or what), a verb (action), and an object (receiver of the action) when needed. For example, "The dog barks."

- Sentence Expansion: As you gain confidence, gradually add details to your sentences using adverbs (describes how), adjectives (describes what), and prepositional phrases (shows location or relationship). For example, "The playful dog barks happily at the mail carrier."

- Vary Your Sentence Length: A mix of short and long sentences keeps your communication interesting and avoids monotony.

3. Enhancing Communication Clarity:

- Know Your Audience: Consider who you're communicating with and tailor your language accordingly. Use simpler terms for younger audiences or those unfamiliar with the topic.

- Focus on the Main Message: Avoid rambling or going off on tangents. Clearly identify your main point and stick to it.

Part 4: Expanding Language Skills in the Autistic Brain
Chapter 15: Building a Strong Foundation for Language Development:
15.3- Cover foundational skills like building vocabulary, using simple sentence structures, and improving communication clarity.

- Organization is Key: Structure your thoughts logically. If writing, use paragraphs with clear transitions to connect ideas. In conversation, use phrases like "first," "second," or "finally" to guide the listener.

- Be Specific: Instead of saying "stuff," identify the specific objects you're referring to. This avoids confusion and ensures your message is understood clearly.

Remember:

- Practice Makes Perfect: The more you read, write, and converse, the more comfortable you'll become with language.
- Don't be Afraid to Make Mistakes: Everyone makes mistakes. Embrace them as learning opportunities and keep practicing. There's always room for improvement.
- Seek Feedback: Ask a trusted friend or family member to provide feedback on your writing or communication style. This can help you identify areas for improvement.
- By focusing on building vocabulary, mastering simple sentence structures, and striving for clarity, you can significantly enhance your communication skills and effectively connect with others.

Part 4: Expanding Language Skills in the Autistic Brain
Chapter 16: Developing Conversational Skills:

Break down the components of successful conversation for the autistic brain.

The autistic brain can approach conversation differently, and success might involve some additional considerations. Here's a breakdown of the components for a successful conversation, tailored for the autistic mind:

Preparation:

- Know the Topic (if possible): If you know the conversation will revolve around a specific topic, do some research beforehand. This equips you with relevant information and talking points.

- Prepare Conversation Starters: Having a few questions or icebreaker topics in mind can be helpful, especially if initiating conversations is challenging.

During the Conversation:

- Focus on Active Listening: Pay close attention to what the other person is saying. Make eye contact (if comfortable) and nod occasionally to show you're engaged.

- Process Information: Give yourself a moment to process information before responding. It's okay to take a pause to formulate your thoughts.

Part 4: Expanding Language Skills in the Autistic Brain
Chapter 16: Developing Conversational Skills:

- Stick to Strengths: Conversations don't have to follow a rigid structure. If you're more comfortable talking about a particular topic, steer the conversation in that direction, offering your expertise or perspective.

- Literal Interpretations: Some people use figurative language or sarcasm. If something is unclear, politely ask for clarification.

- Visual Supports: If it helps, use visuals like pictures or notes to support your points or remember what you want to say.

Social Nuances:

- Nonverbal Communication: Facial expressions, gestures, and tone of voice can be subtle for some autistic individuals. Pay attention to the speaker's body language for additional cues, and be mindful of your own nonverbal communication.

- Turn-Taking: Conversations are a back-and-forth exchange. Wait for the other person to finish speaking before responding. You can use silence or phrases like "go ahead" to indicate your turn is over.

- Managing Overstimulation: Social situations can be overwhelming. If you start to feel overloaded, excuse yourself politely and take a short break to regroup.

Part 4: Expanding Language Skills in the Autistic Brain
Chapter 16: Developing Conversational Skills:

Remember:

- Everyone Communicates Differently: Embrace the unique way each person communicates.

- It's a Two-Way Street: Successful conversations involve both listening and responding.

- Be Patient with Yourself: Social interactions take practice. Celebrate small victories and keep working on improving your communication skills.

Additional Tips:

- Find Conversation Partners Who Share Your Interests: Talking about things you're passionate about can make conversations more enjoyable and engaging.

- Practice Social Skills: Role-playing conversations with a trusted friend or therapist can help you practice social skills in a safe and controlled environment.

- Technology Can Help: There are apps and communication tools designed to support people with social communication challenges. Explore these options and see if they can be helpful.

By understanding these components and tailoring your approach, you can navigate conversations with more confidence and connect with others on a deeper level.

Part 4: Expanding Language Skills in the Autistic Brain
Chapter 16: Developing Conversational Skills:
16.1- Offer strategies for initiating and maintaining conversations, including turn-taking and active listening skills.

Starting and maintaining conversations can feel daunting, but with a few strategies in your arsenal, you can become a confident conversationalist. Here's a breakdown of key tactics to initiate, actively listen, and ensure smooth turn-taking:

Initiating Conversations:

- Observe and Find Common Ground: Pay attention to your surroundings and the people around you. Are they reading a book you recognize? Wearing a cool band t-shirt? Use these as conversation starters! "Hey, I love that book too!" or "Cool band shirt! Have you seen them live?"

- Open-Ended Questions: Instead of questions with yes/no answers, ask open-ended questions that invite conversation. "What did you think of the movie?" or "How was your weekend?"

- Compliments are a Classic: A genuine compliment can be a great way to break the ice. "That scarf looks great on you!" or "I love your haircut!"

Part 4: Expanding Language Skills in the Autistic Brain
Chapter 16: Developing Conversational Skills:
16.1- Offer strategies for initiating and maintaining conversations, including turn-taking and active listening skills.

Active Listening:

- Give Your Full Attention: Put away your phone, make eye contact (if comfortable), and focus on the speaker. Show you're engaged through nonverbal cues like nodding or smiling.

- Ask Clarifying Questions: If something is unclear, don't hesitate to ask questions for better understanding. "So, you're saying..." or "Can you elaborate on that?"

- Summarize and Reflect: Briefly summarize what you heard to show you're paying attention and to ensure understanding. "So, if I understand correctly..."

Turn-Taking:

- Silence Isn't Awkward: Allow a beat after someone finishes speaking before jumping in. A brief pause is natural and allows the other person to elaborate or formulate their next thought.

- Nonverbal Cues: Pay attention to body language and facial expressions. A furrowed brow might indicate confusion and need for clarification, while a leaning forward might suggest the other person is eager to add something.

Part 4: Expanding Language Skills in the Autistic Brain
Chapter 16: Developing Conversational Skills:
16.1- Offer strategies for initiating and maintaining conversations, including turn-taking and active listening skills.

- Transition Phrases: Use phrases like "That reminds me..." or "On another note..." to smoothly shift the conversation and signal it's your turn to speak.

Remember:

- Be Yourself: People are drawn to genuine personalities. Let your unique voice and interests shine through.

- Practice Makes Perfect: The more you converse, the more comfortable you'll become. Don't be discouraged by initial awkwardness.

- Focus on the Journey, Not the Destination: Enjoy the process of getting to know someone and learning new things. Don't put too much pressure on yourself to have a perfect conversation.

- Bonus Tip: Having a few conversation starter topics in your back pocket can be a safety net, especially in unfamiliar situations. Think about current events, hobbies, or interesting things you've seen or heard lately.

By implementing these strategies, you can initiate conversations with confidence, actively listen to others, and ensure smooth turn-taking, fostering meaningful connections and leaving a positive impression.

Part 4: Expanding Language Skills in the Autistic Brain

Chapter 16: Developing Conversational Skills:

16.2- Discuss techniques for understanding nonverbal cues and using them appropriately in conversation.

Nonverbal cues are the silent language of communication, encompassing facial expressions, body language, posture, tone of voice, and even silence itself. While these cues can vary across cultures, understanding and using them effectively can significantly enhance your conversations. Here are some techniques to decipher and utilize nonverbal cues:

Reading Nonverbal Cues:

- Observe Facial Expressions: A raised eyebrow might indicate confusion, a furrowed brow could mean concentration, and a smile (genuine or not) suggests happiness. Pay attention to the overall facial expression and not just isolated features.

- Body Language Matters: Crossed arms can signal defensiveness, open arms can portray receptiveness, and fidgeting might indicate nervousness. Consider the context and body language as a whole for better interpretation.

- Listen Beyond Words: The tone of voice can convey a multitude of emotions. A monotone voice might suggest boredom, while an enthusiastic tone reflects excitement. Listen for changes in pitch and volume.

- Silence Speaks Volumes: Silence can be a powerful cue. A comfortable silence can indicate mutual understanding, while an awkward silence might signal confusion or a need to fill the gap.

Part 4: Expanding Language Skills in the Autistic Brain
Chapter 16: Developing Conversational Skills:
16.2- Discuss techniques for understanding nonverbal cues and using them appropriately in conversation.

Using Nonverbal Cues Appropriately:

- Maintain Eye Contact: Eye contact shows attentiveness and interest. However, be mindful of cultural norms, as excessive eye contact can be seen as disrespectful in some cultures.

- Mirror Subtly: Mirroring body language can build rapport and subconsciously signal that you're on the same page. However, avoid mimicking too obviously, as it can appear inauthentic.

- Smile Genuinely: A genuine smile can put others at ease and create a warm atmosphere. A forced smile can have the opposite effect.

- Project Confidence: Stand tall with open posture (not rigid) to project confidence and engagement. Avoid slouching, which might convey disinterest or boredom.

- Match the Energy Level: If someone is speaking excitedly, mirror their enthusiasm with your tone and body language. If they're speaking softly, adjust your volume accordingly.

Part 4: Expanding Language Skills in the Autistic Brain
Chapter 16: Developing Conversational Skills:
16.2- Discuss techniques for understanding nonverbal cues and using them appropriately in conversation.

Remember:

- Context is Key: Nonverbal cues can have different meanings depending on the context. Consider the situation, the topic of conversation, and the relationship between the people involved.

- Not Always Literal: Nonverbal cues can be ambiguous. Don't rely solely on them to interpret someone's message. Look for consistency between nonverbal and verbal cues.

- Cultural Awareness: Be mindful of cultural differences in nonverbal communication. A thumbs-up might be a positive sign in one culture but offensive in another.

By honing your observation skills and using nonverbal cues strategically, you can become a more effective communicator, building stronger connections and navigating social situations with greater confidence.

In Conclusion:

This book has explored a variety of topics relevant to understanding and appreciating autism spectrum disorder. We've delved into the importance of essential nutrients for overall health, looked at different learning styles, and unpacked the power of communication through active listening, strong vocabulary, and clear expression.

Throughout these discussions, one thing remains clear: people with ASD possess unique strengths and talents that deserve recognition and celebration.

- Their brains process information differently, which can lead to exceptional focus, a keen eye for detail, and a mastery of specific subjects.

- Their honesty and directness can be refreshing in a world of social ambiguity.

- Their ability to think creatively and solve problems outside the box can lead to innovative solutions.

- By creating supportive environments, fostering open communication, and celebrating their unique strengths, we can empower people with ASD to thrive and reach their full potential. This isn't just about overcoming challenges, but about appreciating the remarkable strengths and perspectives that autistic individuals bring to our world.

In Conclusion:

Remember:

- Autism is a spectrum, and every person's experience is unique.

- Early intervention and ongoing support are crucial for maximizing a child's potential.

- With understanding and acceptance, we can create a more inclusive world where everyone can flourish.

- Together, let's celebrate the amazing strengths and contributions of people with ASD!

Printed in Great Britain
by Amazon